LIVING BETWEEN ALPHA & OMEGA

Praying the Greek Alphabet in Uncertain Times

Stella Zuniga Burkhalter

With gratitude for all those who have helped me survive in the in-between, especially Hunter, Wyatt, and Emery, and my sisters and nieces who encouraged me to run with this.

Thanks (and perhaps apologies) to my Biblical language professors at Austin Presbyterian Theological Seminary, John Alsup, John Ahn, and Andy Dearman.

LIVING BETWEEN ALPHA AND OMEGA:

PRAYING THE GREEK ALPHABET IN UNCERTAIN TIMES

Written and Illustrated by Stella Zuniga Burkhalter

Cover design by Emery Burkhalter

Copyright © 2020

Author Website: www.pastorstella.net

Scripture citations are New Revised Standard Version

Printed in the United States of America.

ISBN: 978-x-xx-xxxxxx-x

I am the Alpha and the Omega, the Beginning and
the End, the First and the Last.

– Revelation 22:13

Prologue

"Give me a word, any word, and I will show you how the root of that word is Greek!"

- Gus Portocali, "My Big Fat Greek Wedding"

When I was little, we didn't have a lot of children's books in the house, but we did have three sets of encyclopedias. (My mom wasn't good at running off travelling salesmen.) I remember long summer days spent flipping through World Books, fascinated at the entries with the line drawings showing the evolution of each letter of the alphabet.

Later, in high school, I took a class focused on Greek and Latin root words. Like the father on "My Big Fat Greek Wedding," I could tell you the root words of many English words and parrot them back for a test, though I couldn't fathom why I needed this information. (Thanks for your patience, Mrs. Dovalina.) Then, in seminary, a light came on when I studied Biblical Greek and Hebrew. I found a richness in Scripture that I hadn't had access to before. Because I grew up with a little Spanish mixed in with my English, I have always been able to appreciate how certain words can't be adequately translated. When you add a layer of spiritual meaning, the difference becomes even more pronounced. All of a sudden, words like "glory" and "steadfast" became delicious.

In that season, I found a beautiful book, *The Hebrew Alphabet, a Mystical Journey*.[2] The book invited me to mediate on letters as a spiritual practice. I learned the letters themselves have stories, and I was drawn deeper into the castle. The alphabet became my friend. Now I frequently find myself "praying a letter" as short-hand between me and God. I have not found such a book in Greek, so I decided there needed to be one. Here it is.

---

[2] *The Hebrew Alphabet, A Mystical Journey* by Edward Hoffman (Chronicle Books, 1998)

Contents

Introduction

Life moves fast, and so we often find ourselves rushing from one thing to the next, impatient to check the next thing off the list. We're focused on a destination, and we convince ourselves that happiness and fulfillment lie just beyond the next milestone.

"I'll be happy when....", "I'll be content if...", "I can finally be at peace when...".

But if God is the Alpha and the Omega, the Beginning and the End, we're constrained to be somewhere in the middle, with a good God forever bookending our existence.

That thought can give comfort to the anxious and restless among us. If you're in the middle, you're not behind. You're where you're supposed to be. And if this is where God put you, there must be something for you here. After all, the good stuff usually happens somewhere in the middle, when we least expect it.

Taking a cue from Jesus' statement in Revelation, this book uses the Greek alphabet - from alpha to omega - to spark meditations. Each chapter is intended to offer Biblical insights and encouragement for living in in-between times. Each letter begins a Greek word from Scripture and presents a concept that can give us hope. There are prayer practices to try, Scripture passages to carry, and art to guide your meditation.

The Greek alphabet is one of several incarnations of an alphabet that has evolved over centuries. From the earliest cave drawings, to Egyptian hieroglyphics and Phoenician letters, Greek letters came. Hebrew letters evolved alongside. Eventually, the Roman letters we use evolved from these. During the time of Jesus (who spoke a Hebrew derivative called Aramaic), Greek became the language of the speaking and writing world, and eventually the language of the New Testament. Digging down to Biblical words in their original language and pondering the corresponding Greek letters can give a focus to prayer. Words that may have lost their power through overuse in our native language can take on new life. May it be so for you.

There are 24 letters in the Greek alphabet. Depending on when Easter falls, there can be that many weeks between Pentecost (the end of the Easter Season) and Advent (the lead-in to Christmas), a period the church calls Ordinary Time. The word "ordinary" sounds, well, ordinary, but it comes from the word "ordinal," which means "counted," so this is counted time in the church year, marking our days in rhythm with God.

You have in this book a collection of meditations with a letter a week to help get you through the lull of Ordinary Time, or read one letter a day during a seemingly endless hot summer month, read randomly any time you feel restless waiting.

Breathe in Strength, Breathe out Praise

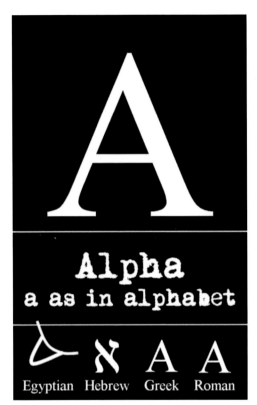

Alpha
a as in alphabet

Egyptian Hebrew Greek Roman

The Greek letter alpha corresponds to our letter A. It began its life as an Egyptian hieroglyph of an ox head. Turn the letter upside down and you might be better able to visualize it. Alpha means "first," and in zoology it designates the dominant animal of the pack, the strongest and most powerful one. Alpha begins the prefix *arch* which means "first" or "top," as in "archangel" or *archiereus,* "chief priest."

Often in Biblical Greek, "A" words are preceded by a breath, a "hu-" sound, so that even though they begin with A in Greek, we write them with an H in English when we transliterate them. This is the case with the word for holy, *hagios,* which starts with alpha in Greek. If we are to begin at the beginning, this is a great first word on which we can focus.

Holiness gets a bad rap sometimes, and the phrase "holier than thou" is an insult. It might help to think of holy as "set aside for a special purpose," rather than simply "correct." Holiness is the goal of all who follow Christ; not an impossible ideal, but a precious purpose.

Make a Connection Both the prophet Isaiah and the author of the Book of Revelation, John, were given visions of heaven. They reported that the spiritual beings continually sing a song to God, "Holy, holy, holy..." Before you ever were, that song was sung, and after you cease to be, the song will continue to be sung. During the short breath that is your lifetime, you may get moments where your spirit falls into harmony with the universe and you sing along.

One of those places is the communion table. During communion, we "join in the eternal hymn," as the liturgy says, and then we all say (or sing) "Holy, holy, holy, Lord, God of power and might, heaven and earth are filled with your glory. Hosanna in the Highest..." Let's think about that for a minute. Somewhere in a realm beyond us, supernatural beings are so captivated with the One at the center that all they can do is repeat with awe, "Holy holy holy!" We get tiny little windows in worship when we get to join the heartbeat of all of creation and all of heaven.

"Holy, holy, holy!" Don't all those "ohs" sound like a longing wail? In Greek it's, *hagios, hagios, hagios,* which sounds like panting for God like a deer pants for water. In Hebrew, it's *kadosh, kadosh, kadosh,* which sounds like the rush and hiss of the ocean tide, or the brush of wings. In Latin, *sanctus, sanctus sanctus* is like a shaking percussion instrument. Imagine what it will be like in the throne room of heaven when we will all sing in our own languages!

Holy, holy, holy is the Lord God Almighty, who was and is and is to come! -Revelation 4:8

Try a Prayer Practice When we are stuck in in-between places, waiting for life to unfold, we often grow anxious or disillusioned. Alpha can refocus us on the fact that God is first and worthy of our praise. We can trust God with our future.

So meditate on alpha for a while. Think about the strong, angular ox-head shape and consider that God is your strength.

Repeat "Holy, holy, holy" over and over again. Some use the term "breath prayer" for a prayer you can say in one breath. Let "Holy, holy, holy" be a breath prayer for you as you begin this book. Breathe in "Holy, holy, holy." Breathe out "Holy, holy, holy." Breathe in strength, breathe out praise. Take the focus off yourself and what you need, and let all your attention be on God. Try to do this throughout the day and let it reorient you. Pant it in Greek, *hagios, hagios, hagios,* sway to it in Hebrew, *kadosh, kadosh, kadosh*, or tremble to it in Latin, s*anctus,* s*anctus* s*anctus*. Join the orchestra.

Climb in, Safe and Secure

Beta

b as in base

Phoenician Hebrew Greek Roman

Letter B originated as a boxy symbol for a shelter. In Hebrew, it became the letter *beit*, which can also be pronounced *beth*. This literally means "home" or "house." And so, for instance, Bethlehem means "house of bread," the place where Jesus, the Bread of Life, was born. The Hebrew letter looks like a little home, with a protective covering over it. The Greeks call their version of the letter beta.

Make a Connection In architecture, the word "basilica" is used for those grand cathedrals that look like castles. The related word *basilea* is Greek for "kingdom" or "reign." In the Bible, Jesus often refers to the Kingdom of God or the Kingdom of Heaven. We can picture this as some perfect place with castles that we will go to when we die, but Jesus often said, "The Kingdom is near." He seemed to speak of it as more of a spiritual state than a physical place.

It's nice to imagine the deluxe suite waiting for us in the clouds, but Revelation 21:3 says, "See, the home of God is among mortals. He will dwell with them; they will be his peoples, and God himself will be with them." Home is not a far-off dream. It is anywhere we are with God. The Kingdom of God is a realm where God's will is done, where there is no suffering or pain, and every tear is wiped away. We get glimpses of that on earth.

Jesus told many parables to help his followers understand the nature of the Kingdom of God. He said it's mysterious, like a seed that is cast to the ground and becomes a plant. He said it's hidden and greatly valuable like a secret treasure. He said it has unseen potential like a tiny mustard seed that becomes a great tree.

The Kingdom of God is our true home, the place we belong, safe beyond the clutches of sin and death. If you feel out-of-place at times, it may help to consider that because you have experienced the feeling of true home, moments of love and perfection, you long to return there. Augustine said we are restless until we find our rest in God. When this broken home on earth feels all wrong, something in us longs to make it right, or just run away toward a better place. Thankfully, there is a better place. Jesus told the disciples, "In my father's house there are many rooms... I go to prepare a place for you." (John 14:2)

Truly, I say to you, whoever does not receive the Kingdom of God as a little child will never enter it. - Mark 10:15

Try a Prayer Practice   When we're living in-between homes or jobs or relationships, we feel as if we are free-floating. And while that may be inevitable in the physical sense, it doesn't have to be so in the spiritual sense. Prayer can transport us to that at-home feeling, secure in the lap of our loving creator.

Remember when you were a child and you would make forts out of blankets or oversized cardboard boxes? You could create a little domain for yourself that felt safe and inviting. Now look at beta with its cozy compartments. Go ahead, imagine yourself climbing in. God has a room reserved for you in the Kingdom, so maybe you can remind yourself of that right now. Check in for a while. Let yourself feel snuggled in, like a fox in its warm den.

7

Hold beta in your imagination. Jesus said the Kingdom is near and invited us to enter it in a childlike way, so run to that spiritual hiding place and crawl back in whenever you feel disoriented.

What are You Becoming?

Gamma

g as in grow

Phoenician Hebrew Greek Roman

Maybe when you think "gamma," you think of sci-fi movies and electromagnetic radiation. Gamma isn't just a term from a B-movie, it's the Greek letter G. Both our letters C and G evolved from this letter, which is why it comes third in line in the Greek alphabet. In an early alphabet, G was a hook said to represent a camel's head.

In Hebrew, G looks like a little sprouting plant, and the same is true for the lowercase form in Greek (γ). This is helpful because gamma begins many words that have to do with birth and growth like *genomai*, "generation," and *genemenos*, "becoming." We can hear it in our word "generate." Gamma also begins the common word *gar*, "because," allowing us to speak about cause and effect.

Make a Connection In the Biblical genealogy of Christ found in the Gospel of Matthew, the word *egennesen* appears over and over. We translate this word as "begat" or "gave birth to" and it connects a long list of fathers and sons. Then a handful of women are grafted in unexpectedly. There's the prostitute Rahab, the poor widow Ruth, Tamar, who had sex with her father-in-law, and Bathsheba who was caught up in adultery with the lustful king, reminding us that God uses all sorts of unlikely people in the grand plan.

9

God incorporates us into his plans and makes us co-creators. In the second letter to the Corinthians, Paul reminds the early Christians how important they are. "You are ambassadors for Christ!" he says. God is seeking to reconcile the whole world, to bring everyone out of a broken relationship, and to restore all creation. And God is doing this by speaking to the lost and discouraged through YOU. What an amazing honor this is! Beautiful new relationships are growing, and YOU get to help grow them by sharing what you know and have experienced and by offering encouragement along the way.

Often, when we are waiting for things to happen, or feeling dissatisfied with where we are, we don't realize how much growing is happening in us and around us. Like dough that needs to rise and bread that needs to bake, sometimes situations just need time. Things may be happening that we can't perceive, just as we can't actually see a plant grow without time-lapse photography. When we're preoccupied with how things need to work out or what needs to happen next, we miss what's happening now. Jesus compared the Kingdom of God to a farmer placing seeds in the ground and somehow, without any effort from him, they grow. (Mark 4:26-29) We humans can provide fertile conditions, but we aren't the ones who cause the growth, God is.

So we are ambassadors for Christ, since God is making his appeal through us: we entreat you on behalf of Christ, be reconciled to God! -2 Corinthians 5:20

Try a Prayer Practice Meditate on the letter gamma and praise God who makes things grow. Thank God who made you grow - from two unique cells in your mother's womb, into a human person with blood and bones and skin and hair, into an adult who can read and speak and reason. Don't miss the marvel of this. Acknowledge the wonder and consider what God may be growing in you even as you read this. As an act of prayer, make something today. Make a meal or bake some bread. Paint a picture or build something. Write a poem or song or love letter. Remind yourself that you are made in the image of God, which makes you a creator, too.

Praise God,
from Whom all Blessings Flow

Delta

d as in delta

Egyptian Hebrew Greek Roman

The Greek letter D is called delta. It began its evolution as a square with a taller side to represent a doorway. Hebrews made this doorway one-sided and called it *daled,* which means doorway. Greeks shaped it like a triangle and called it delta, therefore we use that word to name the triangle-shaped area formed by a branching river and its sediment. Scientists use delta's triangle symbol to designate a change or set of changes, so the word "delta" literally means difference or change.

Make a Connection A change symbol is a good one for the life of faith and for living in the unknown. When you are living in the in-between, you long for positive change and dread that you might be descending into negative change from which you won't be able to emerge. When we struggle with the depressing sameness of life, we need to be reminded of the positive change that God can bring. We need to be reminded of our human potential in the Potter's hands.

Our God is the change business. He changed a handful of dust into a man when he breathed the breath of life into it, he changed a pile of dry bones into a living thing of sinew and muscle and flesh in Jeremiah's vision, and when Jesus walked the earth, he changed people whose skin was covered with leprous sores into whole and healed rejoicing people, to name just a few examples.

Jesus was changed at the transfiguration so that his disciples could get a glimpse of him in brilliant radiance before he began the journey to the cross. What a wonder to imagine what we will be like when we are transformed like this, too. Praise God for good change.

[Jesus] was transfigured before them, and his face shone like the sun, and his clothes became dazzling white.
-Matthew 17:2

Try a Prayer Practice Delta is a good letter to meditate upon because its very shape allows us to imagine things turning around. Think of the icon on a screen saver where a logo bounces from wall to wall on your computer screen in a triangle pattern. You may feel like your life is careening fast in a bad direction, but just like that - ping! - things can change and you can bounce into a completely new trajectory. It's that way with God.

There are some churchy words we say, and we never bother to find out what they mean. Doxology is one of them. If you have spent any time in a traditional church, you could be forgiven if you think Doxology is simply the proper name of the song that goes, "Praise God from whom all blessings flow. Praise God all creatures here below. Praise God above ye heavenly host. Praise Father, Son and Holy Ghost. Amen." *Doxa* is the Greek word used in the Bible to mean "praise," so a doxology is a bunch of praise words strung together.

As a prayer practice, picture the triangle of delta as you say a doxology, a few words of praise for the God who can move mountains. Sing the traditional one or make up your own. Imagine your life changing for the better. Imagine yourself pinging around and going fast in a new and very good direction. Sing "Praise God from whom all blessings flow," and concentrate on the *flow* part. Imagine new and exciting possibilities flowing into your life, bringing light, with your face and clothes shining like Jesus' as you reflect back his goodness.

What Else do You See?

Epsilon
e as in temple

Egyptian Hebrew Greek Roman

The letter E in Greek is called epsilon, and it begins the prefix ex- which means "out of" or "from." Think of "exhale" or of "exclaim," in which breath or words come out of you. It also begins a word that is very common in the Bible, *eidon,* which means "I see."

Eidon is sometimes also translated as "I perceive," because when the Bible uses this word, there's often more going on than what meets the eye.

Make a Connection   In the Book of Revelation, *eidon* appears a lot. The author, John, continually says, "I saw…" as he describes his vision of heaven and the future. What a wonder that a man who was imprisoned for this faith in Christ, a man exiled in a jail cell on the island of Patmos, who likely only had a tiny slit of a window to look through, saw more than any human in history has ever seen.

God does this. God shows things to us that can't be seen with human eyes. We receive the gift of understanding and perceiving beyond our context to the greater story that God is writing. We realize that there's more to life than what we're seeing.

The letter epsilon begins the word *eremos,* which we translate as "desert" or "wilderness." The greatest vision has often come to those alone in deserted places. In the wilderness, Moses saw a burning bush, Jacob wrestled with God, and Jesus was tempted - confronting the many ways the enemy was trying to pull him away from his mission. In some traditions, people go on vision quests, retreats alone into nature, during transition from adolescence into adulthood or in other seasons of change. We all need time during great shifts to grieve, to process trauma, or develop vision for the next phase. We see better when we have some perspective. We have to get out of our own heads.

After this I looked, and the temple of the tabernacle of witness in heaven was opened. – Revelation 15:5.

Try a Prayer Practice If you feel like you are walking through a desert time in your life, focus your spiritual vision and ask God to give you insight into your past or a glimpse of what your future could be like. Looking at a single letter E might remind you of looking at a vision chart. Without my glasses, the E is the only letter I can see on those charts. It's the clearest and most certain at least. Maybe it's the same for you. So start by thinking of the good things you can see for certain in your life. What is as clear as a giant letter E on a vision chart? What do you know for sure about God, about God's love for you, and about your life? Make a list.

Now, just as you have to work a little harder to make out the smaller letters on a vision chart, I encourage you to strain a bit spiritually and try to see blessings that may be less obvious. Impatience has a way of making us short-sighted, which is why we have to work at this. (I was serious about making the list.)

Once you have a list of blessings down, what else is coming into focus? For what do you need to be grateful?

When you think about your blessings, ask yourself, toward what do you need to move? How can you spend more time close to good things so they will be as big as that letter E in your field of vision? How can you distance yourself from negativity, worry, fear, and ugliness so that those thoughts become smaller and smaller and smaller – until they are faint like those tiny words you strain to see on your eye doctor's vision chart? The things you keep in your field of vision affect your spiritual state.

Stir up a Spark of New Life

What's Z doing so early in this alphabet? It's supposed to be at the end, isn't it? When you learn a new language, even if you're just learning a little, you start to realize that you make assumptions all the time. One of my favorite comedians, Steven Wright, asks in his signature deadpan voice, "Why is the alphabet in that order? Is it because of the song?" It's not a bad question.

So here's zeta, early on in the Greek alphabet. In many English-speaking countries, they call the letter "zed," a clue that it is derived from a letter called zeta. The Hebrews drew the letter as a vertical line with a hook on top and named the letter *zayin*, which means "weapon" or "sword." The zig-zag shape we know resembles the lightning bolt weapon of the Greek god, Zeus.

We can think of zeta as a thunderbolt that brings a jolt of life, for the letter begins the Greek word for "life," *zoe*. *Zoe* can also mean "livelihood," the way you support and sustain yourself. In the Gospel of John, Jesus tells us that he came to bring us life abundant. We long for this. We long for "life that is truly life" (1 Timothy 6:16), life that has meaning and purpose. What is the point of living if life has no meaning?

Make a Connection Living in the in-between can be so monotonous that it feels like the life is drained out of us. If you are grieving or healing, you may not feel like getting out of bed in the morning. Apathy can be a threat to faith and even to life itself. Jesus tells us that he came to bring us life. Drawing near to him gives us awareness and appreciation of the life around us. When people have mountain-top spiritual encounters, they often describe it as feeling truly alive, noticing the beauty of the world around them as if for the first time. So much better than a shot of caffeine.

When Jesus met the woman at the well, he told her that the water she was drawing would only sustain her for a while. Soon she would be thirsty again. He told her that he would give her living water, indicating that God provides more than just physical sustenance, but something that enlivens our spirit. Nothing is going to give us eternal life but a relationship with Christ. Nothing is going to make our lives meaningful if we drift away from him.

I came that they might have life, and have it abundantly.
- John 10:10

Try a Prayer Practice When you are overworked and depleted, you often don't realize how much it is affecting you. How are you doing observing God's command to take Sabbath rest? It's a command, not a suggestion, and there's a reason for that.

Need rejuvenation? Try this: meditate on lightning-bolt zeta and imagine yourself receiving the jolt of life God longs to give you. Imagine yourself electrified with life like Frankenstein's monster. What would that feel like? Now think about the things that give you life. Our physical senses can wake up deadened spiritual senses if we're attentive. How you can bring more of those life-giving experiences into your life? Sometimes it's as simple as doing something physically invigorating and being mindful of the exhilaration you feel. Jump into a cold pool. Run to the park. Play with a child. Eat a taco with habanero sauce. Set your alarm and watch the sun rise. Do something that wakes you up. These kinds of things are more fun when shared. Who do you know who needs this as much as you do? Invite that person to join you in your adventure.

It's a Good Day for a Good Day

Phoenician   Hebrew   Greek   Roman

Eta is the most confusing Greek letter if you speak English. It looks like an H, its name starts with E, and it sounds like a long "a." One way to keep it all straight is to know that in its earliest form, it was a hieroglyph of a chain, then later a ladder that looks like a mash-up of E and H. The Greeks drew the ladder with only one rung and called it eta.

Like a helpful little ladder, eta is an important tool, for, as a vowel it allows us to form many words. It can even stand all by itself as a preposition. Even so, eta rarely runs to the front to start a word. One of the few words that begin with eta is *enera,* which means "day." Our eternal God gives us the gift of the rising and the setting sun, marking our days, helpfully telling us with light, "It's time to sleep now" and, "It's time to wake." Days form units of time that we can mark and measure.

Make a Connection   All of this measuring reminds us that the clock is ticking and we finite beings are always running out of time.   When you are living in the in-between, days become things to get through, speed bumps that slow you down as you head toward the inevitable or the longed-for.   Days can drag and we often miss the value of them; we resist seeing each day as precious.   Or else we live at the other extreme, feeling as

21

if the days are going too fast, as if there is never enough time for all we have to do. When we measure our days incorrectly, without the wisdom of God, they seem too long or too short. What would it be like to find the sweet spot? What would a perfect day feel like?

For God, a thousand years is like one day (Psalm 90:4, 2 Peter 3:8), yet God honors our marking of time and sanctifies certain days. The Bible refers to important days, like the Day of Judgment, festival days, and holy days. God commanded us to set aside these days, showing us that these units of time between sunrise and sunset are set aside for us and they matter. The very space we stand in is made holy by God, for God meets us there.

Teach us to number our days, that we may apply our hearts to wisdom. –Psalm 90:12

Try a Prayer Practice This letter in its Hebrew version, *chet*, has the ladder-rung on top, and it symbolizes life and vitality. It begins the word *chutzpah*, boldness. What if you focused on *living* your days with chutzpah, cherishing them rather than just getting through them?

What if you intentionally let each day surprise you as if it were a gift to unwrap? What will the weather be today and how will it change? Who will you see? What will you learn? What will you do? What opportunities will present themselves if you are paying attention? How will the day change as the hours pass, and how will *you* change?

In those occasions when time doesn't seem to be cooperating with your schedule, it's good to stop, take a breath, and think about who is in control. Whose agenda do the sun and moon follow? Aren't you glad it isn't yours? What would today be like if you cooperated with God? Some have the spiritual practice of setting an intention for each day, guiding them to live each day with greater purpose. It's a powerful practice, but better still would be to seek God's intention for your day.

22

Eta is a little ladder, so as you meditate on this letter today, imagine stepping up and seeing the possibilities for a day lived by God's intention. Ladders can be wobbly, so if this idea makes you hesitate and think, "But I have other stuff to do," challenge yourself to trust that when God calls you to follow, God also provides the time and resources you need. Feel free to test this theory.

Seek the God beyond the Horizon

Theta
Th as in theology

Phoenician Latin Greek English

Theta is a letter we don't have in the English language. It makes a "th" sound and begins the word "God," *theos,* which is why we use the word "theology" for the study of God.

There's a word that means "god" in Hebrew, *elohim.* It's a general term that can be used to name any god. The Hebrew Bible uses another word, *Yahweh,* which is the divine name revealed to Moses. We translate this as "LORD" out of respect for the Jews who do not write out God's proper name or speak it aloud. Next time you notice LORD printed in the Old Testament of your Bible in all capital letters, you'll know it's a stand-in for the divine name. So, stop and marvel. We humans *know God's name*! The Greeks, on the other hand, only have one word for God, just like we do. Therefore the word for God used in the New Testament, *theos,* is like *elohim*; it's more of a title than a name.

Make a Connection Jesus had a name for God, "Father," and he invited us to pray to God with this name. Remember when you were a little child and you discovered that your parents had first names? You didn't dare call them by their given names - that was almost silly, and somehow off-limits to you. Instead, you had other names for your parents, Father and Mother, or

Mom and Dad, titles that were just for you and your siblings to use.

Whether you realize it or not, the name you use in prayer says a lot about how you see God. Perhaps our struggles with prayer are reflected in all these names and titles. How do we talk to God when we don't even know what name to use? Father? God? Lord? Jesus? Holy One?

Perhaps we can find deeper meaning in prayer by turning to the ways by which God is referred in the Bible. How would it feel to address God as "Rock," or "Savior," or even -if we dare - in the way of the mystics, "Lover of my Soul"?

The letter theta is a circle with a line across the middle. To some, this letter looks like the earth and the horizon. Perhaps that is a good way to think of God, beyond the horizon of our imagination; greater, bigger, more wonderful than we can name. Perhaps theta can help us picture God as Jesus did in the parable of the prodigal son, always waiting for us on the horizon, waiting for us to come home, waiting for us to seek him.

But while he was still a long way off, his father saw him and was filled with compassion for him. He ran to his son, threw his arms around him, and kissed him. – Luke 15:20

Try a Prayer Practice Meditate on theta today. Imagine God at the horizon. Which of the many names for God in the Bible can best capture what seems to be beyond your sight? Is God a strong presence, like a rock you grasp and cling to amid raging waves? Warm light that fills your soul? The Lion of Judah that inspires you to be strong? Will you see the God of Abraham and Isaac and Jacob, faithful to you through generations? Will you see Jesus, walking with you like he walked with the two believers on the road to Emmaus? Will you feel the wind of the spirit that blew at creation or came down like fire at Pentecost? Will you sense the energy of living water? Will you see a shepherd ready to cradle you like a sheep in his arms?

25

Will you see the Father from Jesus' story - running to you with great joy, wrapping you in an embrace, welcoming you home with a kiss?

In his vision, Isaiah could only see the edge of God's robe filling the temple, yet it was enough to fill him with awe. (Isaiah 6) *Of course* God is beyond your vision. So just go with your best metaphor today and savor that in prayer.

Celebrate a Small Thing

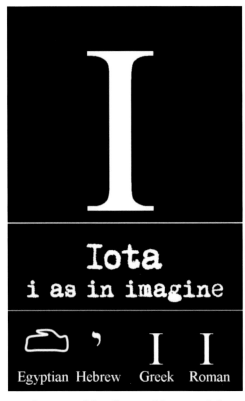

In the Sermon on the Mount, Jesus assured his followers that he would not do away with the law. Matthew 5:18 says, "Until heaven and earth pass away, not one iota, not one stroke of a letter, will pass from the law until everything is accomplished," or as the King James Bible translates it, "not one jot or tittle will pass away." The "iota" or "jot" is the dot on top of the I, and the "stroke" or "tittle" is a horn, or what people who know typeface would call a serif, one of those little "feet" that letters have in certain type styles (like the one you're reading now). In other words, God's law is so trustworthy that not even one tiny dot or foot on a letter will pass away. God cares about details. "Not one iota" has come to mean, "not even the slightest bit." Iota has come to mean a tiny thing, like the dot on an i.

The letter iota began its life as a hieroglyphic of a hand, and gave rise to both the letters I as well as J in English. In Hebrew, the corresponding letter, *yod*, is tiny, just an apostrophe. Because this letter is so small, Jewish mystics have imagined it as a little messenger heralding the first glimpse of something new.

27

Make a Connection Iota begins the Biblical word *idou*, a word we find difficult to translate in English. The King James Bible opts for "Behold!" Other translations say "look" or "see." Ancient writing does not have punctuation. Emphasis is conveyed in the word itself. *Idou* is like that – it's a word that functions as an exclamation mark. In some translations of the Bible where it is found in the original Greek, *idou* is left out entirely and there's punctuation instead. When *idou* appears, either as a word or an exclamation mark, God is trying and catch our attention. He says it when he shows Adam and Eve the trees he's given them in Genesis 1:29, and the Bible uses it at the end of the sixth day of creation when God declared everything he made to be good, Genesis 1:31. And that's just chapter 1. "Behold" appears 1,298 times in its Hebrew and Greek forms!

If we skip all the way to the end of the Bible, we hear Jesus call to us and say, "*Idou*! I am out here knocking on your door, and I will come in and hang out with you if you let me." (My very unofficial translation.)

Behold, I stand at the door and knock. If anyone hears my voice and opens the door, I will come in and eat with him, and he with me. - Revelation 3:20

Try a Prayer Practice In times of uncertainty, hope can be hard to find. If you are feeling a bit hopeless, think of iota. Better yet, think of the dot on top of a lowercase i. When hope appears, it can be so tiny at first, you may not even be sure you're really seeing it, but there it is, making a faint knocking sound at your door, asking to come in. Open the door and behold. Can you detect the slightest bit of forward motion in a situation that has long been stuck?

If you feel like you have no good news to celebrate, look for a small thing, *anything,* a hint of things getting better. Now take that little iota of hope and move on. Moving forward a centimeter is still moving forward. God's got this, and God has a different timetable than you do.

Now think beyond what's concerning you right now and ask yourself what situations that worry you on an ongoing basis. You probably have some pet worries. Most of us do. Is it possible that you have placed yourself in a spiritual state that prevents you from imagining hope in these matters? Listen for a faint knock on the door or your spirit. What might Jesus be wanting to come in and do? You might be missing the message if fears are knocking around in your head.

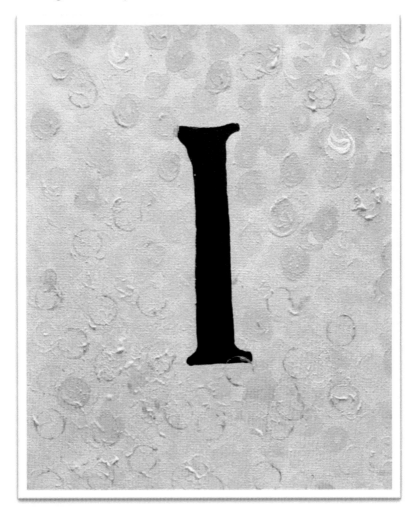

Get on the Beat

Kappa

k as in king

Phoenician Hebrew Greek Roman

The letter we know as K began its life as a symbol for the palm of the hand. For the Phoenicians, the letter was pronged, but the Hebrews shaped it in a loop, more like our capital "C" and called it *kahf,* their word for "palm." The Greeks called it kappa, and gave it a shape like the one we know. This letter can remind us of things at the heart or center, just as the palm is the center of the hand.

The Greek word for "heart" is *kardia,* and so we get our heart-related medical words from it, like cardiac and cardio.

Make a Connection   The heart is at the center of our being. It is the first organ to form in an embryo and the most basic organ that exists in the simplest animal life forms. We tend to think of the heart as the center of emotion, as opposed to the head or brain, which is the center of thought, but for ancient people, this was not so. In Biblical thinking, the heart is the place of the will and intellect. It is the center of morality. The book of Proverbs tells us that evil comes from the heart. King Solomon famously asked for wisdom when offered his greatest wish, but what he actually asked for in the original Hebrew was a *lieb shemah*, a "listening heart." Think about that for a minute – wisdom is not so much a smart brain but a heart that listens. A person in Jesus' day would not understand our expression, "Follow your heart and not your head," for this division of thought and feelings did not exist. Maybe we would do well to fuse these two back together in our imagination as well, realizing that our intellect, our will, and our feelings all come from the same central source.

When the Bible uses the word *kardia,* it refers to the place in your spirit where you feel restless when you are not aligned with God's will for your life. It is the place you hear God speak. It is the place that longs for love. It is the place that breaks. It is the place from which your most profound pain cries out. The Greek word for "cry out," *krazu*, is a kappa word, too, for the deepest cries come from the heart.

In the ancient world, the pumping heart was believed to be the source of the body's heat, and the lungs were thought to cool it. Thus, Jeremiah found God's word to be a fire in his heart that he was weary of holding back. He had to speak out, for God's word was burning in him. (Jeremiah 20:9)

When was the last time you had "heartburn," powerful feelings of restlessness, frustration, anger, or passion? When was the last time you were burning to speak some difficult truth? Often these feelings are the ones we suppress, but they can be signals to which you need to attend. Could it be that you are like Jeremiah, holding back burning fire? Are you weary? Is it time to cry out?

Create in me a clean heart, O God, and renew a right spirit within me. - Psalm 51:10

Try a Prayer Practice Stop throughout your day and put your hand on your heart. Remember that your body has a rhythm and the heart is at the center of your internal circuit driving this rhythm. When you are anxious, your heart races and you may not even realize you are having a physical reaction. So imagine that you can align your heartbeat to God's. As you do so, ask yourself if there is an urgency in your spirit. Try to name what is happening. Do you feel restlessness, frustration, anger, or passion? Pay attention to those feelings. What might God be telling you through them? Is your spirit out of rhythm? What beat is God playing and how can you get in sync?

Use Your Words

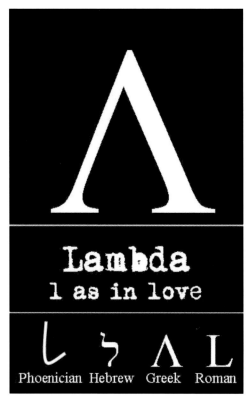

Phoenician   Hebrew   Greek   Roman

This letter originated with the Phoenicians as a hook-shaped ox-goad. The Hebrews and Romans opted to carry on the hook shape, but the Greeks drew theirs more like an upside-down V. The name *lamed* came from Hebrew, and it means both learning and teaching. Perhaps you can imagine a teacher pushing you to the next level of understanding. The Greeks called it something similar, lambda. It begins the word *logos*, which means "word," "saying," or "communication."

Make a Connection   God created the heavens and the earth, and all that is simply by saying, "Let there be…". God said, "Let there be light," and there was light. God said "Let there be animals," and there were animals. God's spoken word, God's spoken will, was all it took to bring the whole universe into being. Words have power.

Mark began his gospel with Jesus appearing in the wilderness and preaching. Luke began his with the events leading up to his birth, Matthew began his with Jesus' ancestry. All of this was written before John ever took pen to parchment, but John needed us to know more. He needed us to know where the Jesus story really started: it started before time. John begins his gospel, his story of the life, passion, and resurrection of Jesus, by saying, "In the beginning was the word, and the word was with God, and the word was God…" In telling the story, he refers to Jesus as "the word," or in Greek, the *logos*. Jesus was the expressed will of God for all creation, the word become flesh.

The Greek word *logos* is so fraught with meaning that some don't even translate it in theological texts, preferring to speak of Jesus as "the Divine Logos," God's expression of love to us, God in a form we can see and hear. We use the word "logo" to mean a visible mark that conveys the brand of a product or company. A logo communicates an image. In that sense, Jesus is God's logo, telling us in visible form who God is.

In the beginning was the Word, and the Word was with God, and the Word was God. –John 1:1

Try a Prayer Practice Lambda originated as a staff used to push an ox. Be with lambda for a while and imagine the prong guiding you by the neck, pushing you to speak, like a farmer might push a reluctant ox to do its work. Might there be something you need to say out loud -to yourself or to someone else? When we remember that God spoke the world into existence, we get an idea of the power of words. How can you use yours? Can you right a wrong, offer encouragement, give a compliment? You might instead imagine God pushing you *not* to speak, saying "Get off that dead-end trail, my little calf." Can you pay more attention to how your words cause damage? Can you pay attention to the ways your well-meaning advice and corrections might come across as demeaning? Can you vow to complain less? Can you use your words to create an opening for someone else to speak up?

This is a lot to think about. If your find yourself frustrated about your inability to control your tongue, or if you're fixated on something you said or didn't say, stop. The past is the past. Here's something constructive you can do now: use your words and write a prayer of worship. You can do this. Don't edit or critique yourself, just write. Write words to hymns. Write thank you words. How many words can you get on paper that say something about who God is? Now look at that - you know a lot of words! You know how to use them. In fact, you may never know all the times that you have used your words well. Count your written prayer as the start to a life in which you bless the world with words.

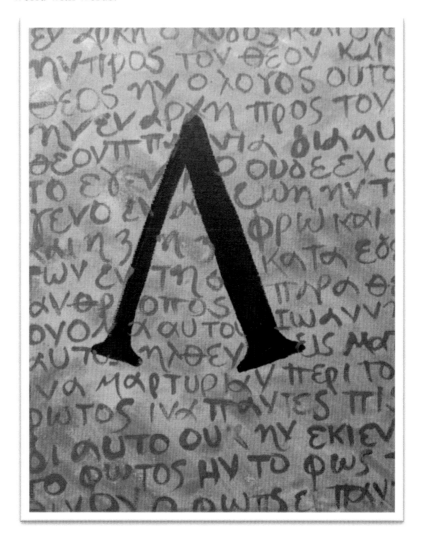

Dive in to the Mystery

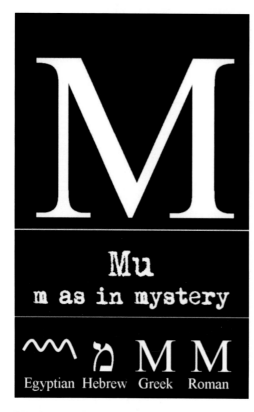

Mu

m as in mystery

Egyptian Hebrew Greek Roman

In English, as well as in earlier Phoenician, Hebrew, and Greek forms, this letter resembles waves and likely began as a symbol for water. The letter is called mu in Greek and it begins the word *mysterion*, "mystery," and *magi,* those mysterious wise men from afar in the Christmas story.

Mu begins the word *mega,* "large," as well as *mathites,* the word for disciples.

Make a Connection Mu can remind us of watery depths that are concealed from view. Think of icebergs that are almost completely submerged, reminding us that there is so much more than what meets the eye. This is a good image for God and for the life of faith. We can imagine ourselves floating in the mysteries of life, with the weight of God's unseen presence mooring us.

When you read through the gospels, it is easy to identify with the disciples, the *mathites,* as they struggle to understand the deep truths Jesus shares with them. Jesus makes God's truth more accessible through parables, but still, people do not understand. In the Gospel of Matthew, chapter 13, Jesus tells the parable of the sower, which he later explains to the disciples. They wonder why he uses parables, and Jesus quotes the words God spoke to the prophet Isaiah, "Seeing, they do not perceive and hearing, they do not listen." And yet, Jesus says, "It is not so with you." You get to understand mysteries. And so he tells them, "Blessed are your eyes, for they see." What an amazing gift! Later, Paul, who was also given insight into the mysteries of God, would tell the believers in Corinth, "Listen, I will tell you a mystery!" and he proceeded to explain death, resurrection, and the second coming of Christ. (I Corinthians 15) What a secret to hear!

We may not understand the mystery of why God is revealed to us and not to others, but we can marvel and praise God for that fact. Who are we that God would let us in on the secrets? Or as the psalmist puts it, "When I consider your heavens, the work of your fingers, the moon and the stars which you have set in place, what is mankind that you are mindful of them, human beings that you visit them? You have made them a little lower than angels and crowned them with glory and honor." (Psalm 8:4-5)

Listen, I will tell you a mystery! We will not all die, but we will all be changed, in a moment, in the twinkling of an eye, at the last trumpet. For the trumpet will sound, and the dead will be raised imperishable, and we will be changed.
– 1 Corinthians 15:51-52

Try a Prayer Practice Find a body water to look at, even if it is just a waterscape in a photograph or painting. Look for the little M's on the surface of the water. Think of the mystery of God and his unfathomable love. Be grateful that you know a little something of this. Sit in that wonder and gratitude for a while. Then imagine diving deeper into the water. Imagine seeing things as God sees them. Imagine your life, the things you worry about, your problems. So far, you've only seen a bit of how things are. That's the tip of the iceberg. Remember that icebergs are much bigger than the bit we see on the surface, so imagine seeing the rest of the iceberg. You have only been looking at the surface of your life, and you may not see what you're looking for. Know that there are unseen things you do not know about yet, the details of the past and future, the massive work of God underneath it all. Come up from the water and recognize that the God of the deep has a much bigger picture of your life and more in store for your future.

Make Friends with the Night

The Egyptians created a symbol for a snake, then the Hebrews turned it into another scaled creature, a fish, and gave it the name *nun,* their word for fish. The Greeks called it nu.

The letter we know as N starts "no" words in many languages – *nyet*, *nada*, nil – a lot of negativity going on there. In Greek, nu begins the word for night, *nuz.* It also begins the word for dead, *nekros*.

Make a Connection   In the Bible and in our lives, important things happen at night. Paul's jailer in the Acts of the Apostles came to know the power of God in the night after an earthquake, when his prisoners saved his life. Nicodemus sought out Jesus under cover of darkness to ask him the deepest question of his soul, the same question asked by the bewildered jailer, "What must I do to be saved?" Peter denied Jesus as he stood by a warming fire in the dead of night. Jesus wept through the night in Gethsemane.

Christian mystic John of the Cross described the "Dark Night of the Soul," a time during which all hope is lost and we discover that in the end, nothing can separate us from the love of Christ, for Jesus is with us, even in the dark depths. This descent to rock-bottom is sometimes what finally opens us to the truth.

Darkness, night, and death are frightening, but they are necessary. Our bodies rest, grow, and heal as we sleep through the night. We conquer our fears when we face them in the darkness. We resurrection people need not fear death, for as Scripture says, "Oh, death, where is your sting?" We will pass through death to eternal life, free from pain and suffering.

We need darkness to appreciate the glory of light; we need night to comprehend the fullness of day. The glory of Easter shines brighter because of the darkness of Good Friday. Embrace the night. See it as an opportunity to be strengthened and to grow. Allow the sadness and the struggles that inevitably come, for joy comes in the morning, made sweeter by the knowledge that we survived the night.

And it came to pass in those days, that [Jesus] went out to the mountain to pray, and he continued all night in prayer to God. –Luke 6:12

Try a Prayer Practice Go out at night and look at the sky. Psalm 74:16 says, "The day is yours, the night also is yours." Night belongs to God, and God has purposes for darkness. Scripture promises that in the end, there will be no night, that God himself will be the light. But that time is not now, and only God knows why. It's here to stay, so make friends with the night.

Little children fight sleep, especially when they are exhausted and need it most. When we are grown up, we give up that fight. We know that sleep will find us, and we let it. We eventually accept that we don't have control in the battle for sleep; we don't even get to choose the moment we fall asleep, it just happens. Think about that when you go to bed tonight. Sleep will come eventually, and you won't have control over it.

What if you could trust so completely in other areas of your life? Think of a situation that is not going as you would like it to. Might your fight in this situation be as useless as fighting sleep at night? Might you need to just let things happen and trust that it will be OK?

Fear of the dark is one of the most common fears. It's a fear of the unknown, a fear of not having control. Practice seeing the beauty in the unknown. Practice trusting the one who knows. Practice worshipping the one who is in control and is completely capable of handling it all. Let the stars remind you that God is so much bigger than you can comprehend.

Spread a Table

Xi

x as in fix

Phoenician   Hebrew   Greek   Roman

Xi is a strange and interesting letter. It makes a "ks" sound and is not used very often in Biblical Greek. Xi is often confused with Greek X (chi) which makes a similar sound. In its uppercase form, it is three horizontal lines, which looks like a Z at first glance. In lowercase form, it is a squiggle that looks like an uppercase cursive E.

Perhaps because it has been so easily confused with other letters, Xi got lost. As alphabets evolved, no one thought Xi was necessary. Xi begins the Greek word, *xinia*, which means "lodging," and when prefixed with *philo-* which means "love" or "fondness," it becomes *philoxinia*, "hospitality." This is an important spiritual discipline that is sometimes also unappreciated.

Make a Connection In the Middle Eastern setting of the Bible, hospitality was vital. People travelled great distances on dangerous roads and relied on the hospitality of those along the way to keep them alive. Throughout the Bible, you see hospitality displayed, such as Abraham welcoming the three visitors into his tent in Genesis 18. In Hebrews 13:2, we're reminded to show hospitality to strangers for, like Abraham, we may be entertaining angels unaware.

In the New Testament, Paul thanks various people for their hospitality and it's clear that this is indispensable to him as he goes about his missionary work. He asks Philemon to prepare a guestroom for him, a *xenian,* indicating that he will come to stay.

The Bible shows us that it's important to offer hospitality, but we also see the importance of receiving it. Jesus travels about with no home of his own, frequently dining at the homes of others. Accepting dinner invitations is a way of accepting others, as Jesus accepted the despised tax collector, Zacchaeus, by letting him know that he would dine at this home. By coming into his house, Jesus came into his life and transformed it. (Luke 19)

We humans are wired for connection, but we are becoming more and more disconnected from each other. It's easy to shelter ourselves in our homes and to believe we have everything we need. As hospitality becomes a lost art, we begin to feel insecure about our ability to share it. Our homes don't seem nice enough to have people over. We're too busy to cook a meal. Think of a time you had dinner at someone's house that was especially enjoyable. It probably wasn't the nicest or neatest house. What makes a gathering special is the spirit of the host. Hospitality is generosity combined with peace – a host who is frazzled and overly concerned with perfection makes everyone uncomfortable.

Do not neglect to show hospitality to strangers, for by doing so, some have entertained angels without knowing it.
– Hebrews 13:2

Try a Prayer Practice   Hospitality is a dying art. If you've enclosed yourself a little bit, crawl out and take the risk of spreading a table for someone. Invite someone over for dinner or call an out of town friend to come stay with you for a weekend. Think about being generous and peaceful. Think about truly enjoying the company of another person, even if everything is not perfect.

Serving may not seem like a prayer practice, but make it one. Pray as you prepare for your guest, thanking God for the person. Consider how you have seen the image of God reflected in your friend and marvel at the God who meets us in the face of another. If opening your home is not possible now, start with a phone call.

Imagine There's a Heaven

There are two O's in the Greek alphabet. The first makes a small O sound, so it's called omicron because "micro" is the Greek word for "small." The other O makes a bigger sound, so it's called omega. Mega means "big."

The Egyptians drew a symbol of an eye which was adopted by the Hebrews who called it by their word for eye, *ayin*. The Phoenicians rounded and simplified the shape into a simple circle, which the Greeks adopted as omicron and passed on to us.

Omicron begins the word *oikos* which means "house" or "home," and *oranos*, which means "heaven," our true home. You can imagine the round space as a shelter, or even a womb.

Make a Connection In the Book of Revelation, John was given a vision of heaven. He describes it in rich and shimmering hues, with rainbows and bright, dazzling light. There are all sorts of glistening precious stones and lush trees with leaves that bring healing. John saw a multitude of people from all nations and saw a New Jerusalem, a holy city, coming down to earth. He described magnificent structures, gates made of pearl and streets made of gold. The prophet Isaiah saw the beauty of heaven, too, and said lions and lambs would lie together and all creation would be at peace. Heaven is described as a place of beauty and peace, as well as a place of feasting and singing.

After this, I looked, and there was a great multitude that no one could count, from every nation, from all tribes and peoples and languages, standing before the throne and before the lamb, robed in white, with palm branches in their hands. – Revelation 7:9

Try a Prayer Practice You're not alone if you tend to avoid the Book of Revelation, for its mysterious and frightening creatures and symbols confuse a lot of us, but the artists among us have always gravitated to it. Its verses have inspired countless songs, paintings, poems, and stories. The imagination can grasp it better than the intellect, and the bizarre nature is more of a draw to artists than it is a hindrance.

If you find yourself in an in-between place, struggling to find peace, perhaps it would help to stop thinking about where you are and start dreaming of where you will be. If you need inspiration, call in an artist. Find a song or picture or movie that seems heavenly to you. Flip through Revelation and look for passages that describe the beauty of the place.

Consider the wide-open possibilities suggested by the letter O, that big, all-seeing eye. Imagine you're a movie-maker setting up a scene of heaven. Forget the typical scenes of fat baby cherubs floating in the clouds with harps. Instead, consider what perfect beauty might look like. What would heaven include if it had the best of everything? What would people be doing there? What would *you* be doing there?

It's easy to get carried away imagining the endless buffet and non-stop pleasure, but if you consider what it would really be like to live in heaven, you might realize that you get to do some heavenly things here on earth sometimes. Are you enjoying those things lately? Can you try to savor more?

What if you decided to set aside time every day for heaven practice? If you're going to spend eternity there, you might as well start getting good at it. Maybe you could sing more. Or talk to Jesus the way you'd imagine doing when you're face to face. The Bible says we'll be with people from every nation on earth. Can you find some people to worship with who bring a different flavors and experiences than what you're used to? And what if you made it a priority to take communion, a foretaste of the heavenly banquet? Make house calls on God every once in a while.

Breathe in the Spirit

Pi

p as in peace

Egyptian Hebrew Greek Roman

The earliest people drew a shape to symbolize a mouth, and it came to be associated with the "p" sound. In Hebrew, the letter is shaped like the profile of a face with an open mouth, and it's called *peh*, the word for "mouth." The Greeks changed *peh* to pi and gave it a new shape. We know the word and symbol pi from mathematics. It's the ratio of a circle's circumference to its diameter.

The letter pi begins the word *pneuma*, with a silent "P," which means both "breath" and "spirit," appropriate for a letter that originated as a mouth. When our lungs lose their function, we get pneumonia, a word in which you can still detect the Greek word for breath.

Pi begins the word *paraclete*, a name for the Holy Spirit that literally means, "one who comes alongside" or "advocate." Picture a breeze carrying you along or a gust blowing open a path ahead of you. Pi also begins the word *pistis*, "faith."

Many Biblical passages take on new meaning when we understand that breath and spirit are the same word. In the creation story, we are told that a breath, spirit, or wind from God swept over the waters. (The Hebrew word *ruach* also has this complex meaning.) Those who translate the Bible into English had to settle on one word, missing the richness of the original Biblical languages.

Make a Connection God is as close as the very air we breathe. God breathed life into the first human and Jesus breathed the Holy Spirit onto his disciples. The double meaning of *pneuma* helps us better understand the nature of the Holy Spirit.

In the popular Christian song "Breathe," by Michael W. Smith, the lyrics say, "This is the air I breathe, your holy presence living in me." In the more recent All Sons and Daughters song, "Great are you Lord," we hear, "It's your breath in our lungs, so we pour out our praise to you only." Way before that, back in 1878, Robert Hatch wrote, "Breathe on me Breath of God, fill me with life anew, that I may love what thou dost love, and do what thou wouldst do." In our songs and hymns we remember that God is as near as our very breath. God is within us, intimate enough to know us at the cellular level. What an important statement of faith for those times when we feel God is distant.

When [Jesus] had said this, he breathed onto them and said to them, "Receive the Holy Spirit." –John 20:22

Try a Prayer Practice Practitioners of yoga place great emphasis on the breath. When we aren't at peace, when we're afraid or stressed or angry, our breath is shallow and fast. When we get panicked, we don't breathe deeply enough, depriving our bodies of much-needed oxygen. Controlling and intentionally slowing down the breath helps us control and slow down our emotions.

As you pray today, start by focusing on your breath. Close your eyes and take deep, slow breaths. Imagine you are breathing out all the cares and worries of your day. As you breathe in, imagine the *pneuma hagion*, the Holy Spirit/Holy Breath, filling your body, seeking out the places that need healing, the disturbing memories, regrets, and fears that need to be blown away, the stuffiness that needs a breath of fresh air.

This is a similar prayer practice as with alpha at the beginning of this book. This wordless breath exercise can help calm you when you need it. You might add a "holy, holy, holy" prayer with your breath as you feel yourself filling with the presence of God.

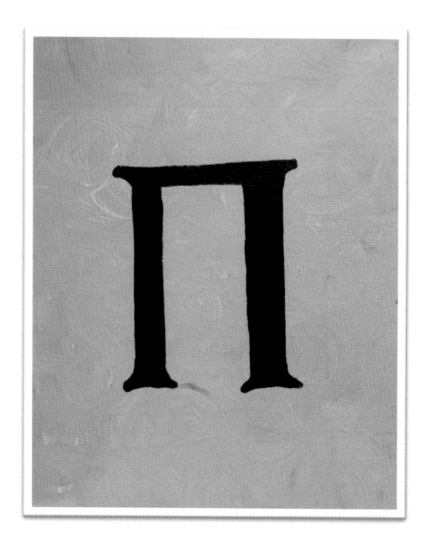

Don't Lose Your Head

Rho
r as in rabbi

Phoenician Hebrew Greek Roman

Early peoples created a symbol for a head, which looks to us like a triangle-shaped flag. It became the curved Hebrew letter *resh*, which means head. The Greeks gave this letter a name that sounds similar, rho, and curled the curve around to form a letter that looks like our letter P. The Romans finished it for us and added the other leg to form our letter R.

Spend some time with rho, and think about what you put at the head of your life.

Make a Connection During the time of Jesus, the primary expression of faith was the Hebrew sacrificial system. You lived your faith by bringing sacrifices to the temple. After the temple was destroyed, a study-focused faith rose to prominence that became the dominant expression of Judaism. The synagogue eclipsed the temple and there was a new way of living faith, a way of digging deep into the Scriptures; a way that was already taking root at the time of Jesus.

Students attached themselves to teachers, calling them *rabbi,* which translates as "my master," or, more precisely, "my head." The New Testament retained this Hebrew word for teacher, a word that doesn't appear in the Hebrew Bible since the practice of studying under a rabbi came to the fore after most of the Hebrew Scriptures were set in stone (or, more likely, set on vellum scrolls).

It seems antiquated to refer to someone as "master." Realizing this makes us aware that we do not easily submit to authority in our time. The word "master" evokes terrible images of slavery and subjugation. We like the idea of Jesus as a friend walking beside us, giving us comfort. The title "master" doesn't fit so comfortably. It seems even crazier to call someone "my head."

So let's set aside the titles of master or head (or even headmaster, with all of its boarding school associations). Let's think about the title rabbi instead. The disciples referred to Jesus as rabbi, which expressed their submission to him. They were drawn to him, dropping their fishing nets and walking away from their tax tables, giving up family and home to follow him. He spoke with authority, and crowds gathered around him so tightly that people had to climb up on the roof and tear in to reach him; he had to float out into the sea in a boat to give himself some breathing room and preaching space. We may resist giving up control, but when something is so alluring, so magnetic, so wonderful, that concern slips away. And so it was with Jesus.

People often speak of not having time for their spiritual lives. They attempt to wedge Jesus into a to-do list, as if he has to compete with doing the laundry and paying bills. How about daring to listen to him as Lord and master, learning from him and letting his teachings dictate your choices as the first disciples did? What if you considered the possibility that in doing so, you might be so drawn in that you'd want nothing but God? The laundry can wait.

Come to me, all you who are weary and carrying heavy burdens, and I will give you rest. Take my yoke upon you and learn from me, for I am gentle and humble in heart, and you will find rest for your souls. For my yoke is easy and my burden is light. – Matthew 11:26-30

Try a Prayer Practice   To us, rho looks like a "P" with a leg missing, When our priorities are set by our selfish desires, we are like a body with a head missing, a chicken with our head cut off. We run around anxious. We get exhausted easily.

Make Jesus, your head, your rabbi. What could that look like for you? How could his priorities be yours? When you wake up in the morning, pause in bed for a moment and pray for Jesus to show you what you need to focus on this day. Is it possible that you have taken on responsibilities that are not yours? Is it possible that busyness is causing you to neglect your purpose?

Love Your Beloved Flesh

Sigma is the Greek letter S. The earliest inscriptions of this letter on rock were written to represent a tooth or tusk. The Hebrew word *shin* means "tooth," and the Semite people drew this letter like our W. The Greeks took the shape and turned it on its side, keeping the "s" sound. From the beginning, sigma has been associated with the body. *Sarx,* the Greek word for "flesh," starts with sigma, as does the word *soma,* which means "body," and *stoma,* which means "mouth." You can tell that our word "stomach" has that as a root. Things are connected in the body.

Make a Connection The apostle Paul made a distinction between the flesh, *sarx,* and the spirit, *pneuma.* The flesh is the part of us with material, selfish desires that does battle against our spiritual side. Paul's description helps us understand our nature as fallen creatures with sinful desires, but it has also historically led to the mistaken belief that our bodies are unholy, dirty, and even evil. God called all things in creation "good," including the human body. Our bodies can experience tastes, sights, and smells that are beautiful and draw us nearer to God.

Our bodies are good and can help us experience good. When the spirit and flesh are in harmony, all is well.

We can call our bodies good because Christ redeemed them by becoming *sarx* himself. By entering into human flesh, God reached down and saved us from ourselves. He made it possible for our bodies to be glorified like his, promising that we would experience resurrection.

Our flesh is what the world sees of us, and sometimes it reveals more than we would like. We get goose bumps when are cold, we sweat when we are nervous, we blush when we are embarrassed. Our skin color says something about who we are and where our ancestors came from. It can be beaten and bruised. What a marvel that the Son of God would take on something so vulnerable.

In explaining resurrection, Paul used the analogy of a tent (Greek *skeinnos* – another sigma word). Our earthly bodies are like tents, flimsy and perishable. We are uncomfortable in these tents, groaning in pain. When we are resurrected, though, our bodies will be like permanent homes, glorified and perfected in ways we cannot imagine. (2 Corinthians 5)

When we live in between alpha and omega, we live in a tent, longing for perfection. It's only tolerable when we trust that perfection will come and that this sometimes vulnerable and uncomfortable state is not forever.

Do you not know that your body is a temple of the Holy Spirit within you, whom you have from God? You are not your own, for you were bought with a price. So glorify God in your body. - 1 Corinthians 6:19-20

Add a Prayer Practice Your flesh is amazing. It grows, heals itself, protects you from infection, cools you off by sweating, and holds you together. Appreciate it. Know that God saved not just some disembodied spirit inside you, but all of you.

We Christians sometimes suffer from disembodied faith and think that the only thing that matters is what we believe. Loving God is more than just what happens in our heads. We sing. We speak. We use our hands to serve. We use our arms to embrace and carry. Rub lotion on your body today and appreciating your *sarx*. Thank God for your body and all the things it can do. Consider all the ways it blesses you. Thank Jesus for becoming flesh and experiencing embodiment with you. Marvel that he was made of the same stuff as you are.

Strive for Perfection

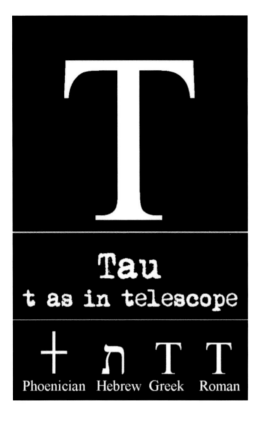

Tau
t as in telescope

Phoenician Hebrew Greek Roman

The letter T hasn't changed much over the centuries, existing as a cross in different alphabets. The Greek letter T is called tau. The letter begins the Greek word *teleos,* "perfection" or better yet, "maturity." It refers to reaching the end of a cycle, or reaching a goal. The words telescope, telegraph, telephone all imply bringing us close to something that is far away. You can think of marking a far away goal with a lowercase "t" hash mark.

Make a Connection Teleology is a doctrine that assumes everything has a reason for being and a purpose. Students of the Bible find that God created the world on purpose. We aren't here because of some cosmic accident or coincidence. We believe that we are designed *for* something.

Jesus understood his purpose – but fulfilling it wasn't easy. He became deeply troubled as the end drew near. When he prayed in the Garden of Gethsemane, Luke tells us that his sweat fell like drops of blood. And yet, he accepted it all and went to the cross. It is the same for us - when we understand our purpose, we can endure discomfort and even pain we may face on the way.

The Bible tells us to be perfect as God is perfect, which sounds like an impossible goal. An understanding of the Greek word for perfect, *teleios*, is helpful. When Jesus tells us to be *teleioi,* he is telling us that we should strive to reach the purpose for which God has created us. We should long to become fully mature. As hard as that is, it's a much more realistic goal.

The Greek word for sin, *hamartia*, is an archery term that means "missing the target." So we can think of sin as messing up, and perfection as hitting the mark, landing right where God has always been pointing us.

Sometimes we forget our purpose and lose our motivation. Paul said to the Romans, "I consider that the suffering of this present age is not worth comparing with the glory about to be revealed to us. We know that all things work together for good for those who love God and who are called according to his purpose." (Romans 8:18 and 28) God has a purpose. You were made on purpose for a purpose. Even if you don't feel you know the purpose of your life, you can live with a purpose today. Each faithful thing you do for God and for the world today is a step in the right direction, and sometimes all you can do is take the next faithful step. Think of T and aim for the target.

Now my soul is troubled, and what shall I say? "Father, save me from this hour?" No, it was for this very reason that I came to this hour. –John 12:27

Try a Prayer Practice Shooting arrows, throwing darts, or even pitching wads of crunched up paper into the trash can help focus our minds on perfection in the Biblical sense.

Do a little throwing today. It may seem silly, but using your body will focus your mind. As you throw, recall the actions of the past day, the past week, the past season. If you want to go deeper, look up the church father Ignatius and his practice of daily self-examination. It's been a meaningful practice for Christians for centuries.

Whether you go deep or just pitch a few projectiles, you may naturally start by thinking about your regrets, your sins. Facing the truth is important. But make sure, in the tradition of Saint. Ignatius, you also examine what you got right. When have you felt close to Christ lately? When were you a disciple? In what ways generally are you hitting the mark in life? In what ways are you growing in skill and self-discipline? A teeny, tiny bit closer to God is still closer. Celebrate that!

It's all Relative

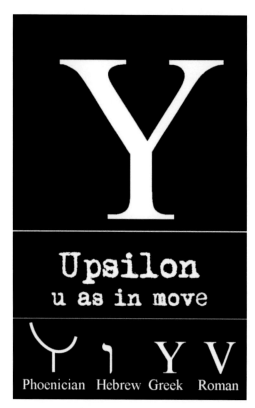

Upsilon
u as in move

Phoenician Hebrew Greek Roman

Our letters U, V, and W all originated from an ancient Egyptian hieroglyph of a tent pole or support hook. The Greek letter upsilon was one step in that evolution. The Greek word *upo* means "under" or "submissive to," and from it we get the prefix hypo- that we find in words like hypodermic, which means "under the skin," as well as hypothermia, a condition in which body temperature is under the normal range.

The Greek word for son is an upsilon word, *uios*, one who appears in the genealogical line under his father. You can hear echoes of it in the Spanish word for son, *hijo*.

Make a Connection We use the symbol of the Trinity to express the relationship between the Father, Son and Holy Spirit, which means that we imagine God as a being who is relationship by definition. Jesus confirmed this; he referred to himself both as the Son of Man and the Son of God, identifying himself in relation to us and to God. He is our connector to God. Through him, we are invited to be one with the Three-in-One.

It's hard to fathom how Jesus could be both Son and God at the same time. Equally shocking is the image of Jesus rolling up his sleeves and kneeling before his disciples to wash their feet. Jesus' existence doing the will of the Father and serving humanity were intrinsic to his identity. He told us that those of us who wish to be like him must become servants. The titles "Son of Man" and "Son of God" bear the marks of sacrificial love.

Jesus not only called us to think of others more highly than we do ourselves, but he also set an example of what this looks like in real life. As we find ourselves in relation to others - as sons, daughters, siblings, coworkers, friends, neighbors. We are expected to live in this way.

The path to which Jesus calls us takes great self-discipline. Relationships are hard to build and easy to break. We have to fight our selfishness and our tendency to pull away from others when we find them difficult. When you are living through an unsettled season, you may click into survival mode and unconsciously decide to become a lone wolf, breaking away from your pack. Your frustration may cause you to lash out at others, and you may become unkind. If those around you are going through difficulties, too, they might do the same. The result is chaos.

Broken relationships lead to broken lives. If you were to walk through a homeless camp and interview the people there, you would find something they have in common is broken relationships. Those suffering in homelessness are almost always estranged from parents, spouses, and siblings. Their spiritual tents have no poles.

Then a cloud overshadowed them, and from the cloud there came a voice, "This is my Son, the Beloved. Listen to him." – Mark 9:7

Add a Prayer Practice   We are made in the image of God, the one who exists eternally connected in relationship, therefore we are wired to be in relationships with others.

Friendships are an important and often overlooked priority. It can be easy to dwell on the ways that others have hurt us or haven't lived up to our expectations. Practice forgiveness, and instead of focusing on what's missing, think about the ways your relationships help you thrive. What are your most meaningful relationships? What can you do today to show gratitude and love? What kinds of relationships are you longing for? How can you nurture a budding relationship, work to repair a broken one, or plant a seed for a new one? How can you be more Christlike in your relationships? How can you reach out to someone who needs support?

Let there be Light

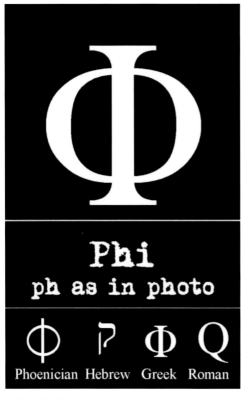

Phi

ph as in photo

Phoenician Hebrew Greek Roman

The letter phi makes a "ph" sound. The early Phoenician symbol evolved into Greek phi and into our modern-day Q, but we don't have a corresponding ph-letter in English. The best we can do to capture this sound in our alphabet is the letter F.

Phi begins the word "light," *phos,* and many of our light-related words carry this as a prefix, like "phosphorescent" and "photo." It might be helpful to think of phi's circle being the earth, and phi's vertical line being a ray of light breaking in from heaven.

Make a Connection Just as the letter phi is not used in our alphabet and therefore has become invisible to us, light is invisible. What we see is the effect of light on everything it touches. Light is a form of energy that gives life. Through photosynthesis, plants make food from sunlight, and we eat plants for food.. Light is a metaphor for God, for we can't see God, but we can see the effect God has on the world.

God causes things to become visible and brings them to light. The Greek word *phaino* can be translated as "appear," "become visible," "reveal," "bring," or "carry." God who is light makes things appear out of nothing. God reveals things that were always there but not perceived before. John refers to Jesus as the light of the world, for he revealed the path to salvation, as well as things we didn't necessarily want to see, our human weaknesses, our selfishness, and our greed.

When we're downcast, we feel like we are under a dark cloud. Light seems to be missing. We use the expression, "Every cloud has a silver lining," but we often have trouble actually believing that platitude. Depression and worry can blind us to many truths, such as the truths that we were created in God's image, we are loved, God is faithful, and God is at work in the world even now answering prayer. The good in the world around us can't be seen without divine light. If we're attentive, though, God can help us detect a trace of hope even when things seem dark.

When people describe experiences with the Holy Spirit, they'll often describe them as "aha moments," times when it seemed a light was suddenly switched on and they saw the truth, or found a creative solution to a problem, or were directed to an answer to a prayer. God turns the light on. Cartoonists draw a light bulb over a person's head to signify these kinds of moments.

It's important for us to remember all of this. On our own, we often lack the ability to see things clearly. We need prayer, we need spiritual discipline, we need God acting though others. We can't reach the switch on our own, and because of that we often go about life assuming there is no switch. This is why we need to prioritize relationships with trusted friends and wise mentors. We need to lean on those who have gone before us and written guides to the life of faith.

In him was life, and that life was the light of all people. The light shines in the darkness, and the darkness did not overcome it. - John 1:4-5

Add a Prayer Practice Pay attention to light. Notice how light affects the world around you. Appreciate the beauty it produces. Candles have been used in prayer and worship for centuries. Notice how a small light can illuminate the darkness. Light a candle as an act of prayer. Think about who has helped you see hope when things looked dark. It's likely that a brief comment or small action made a big difference to you. Appreciate that. Your simple words and actions can be an answer to prayer like that, too. Ask yourself what patches of darkness around you need God's light.

Jesus was a Marked Man

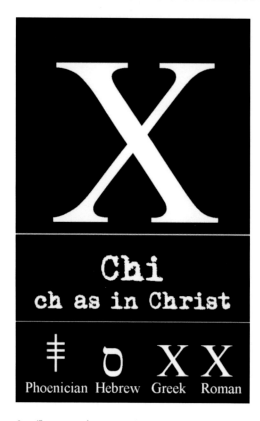

Chi

ch as in Christ

Phoenician Hebrew Greek Roman

The Greek letter chi is shaped like our letter X. It's a cousin of X and the Greek letter xi, for both evolved from the same root letter, which symbolizes a fish or fish bones. Although it looks like our seldom-used letter x, it makes a slightly different sound, and it begins many Greek words, including *christo,* or "Christ." One of the earliest symbols for Jesus was the Greek letters chi and rho superimposed on one another, as these are the first two letters of the name *Christo.*

Some other chi word are *chara,* "joy," and *charis,* which can mean "grace," "gift," or "charity."

Make a Connection Jesus was given the Greek title *christos,* which means "anointed one." "Messiah" is the Hebrew version of the same word.

In ancient times, people were anointed, or ceremonially marked with oil, usually on the forehead, as a way to signify a special status. In the Bible we find that prophets, priests, and kings were anointed. The titles christ and messiah have been used for others, most notably King Cyrus, who allowed the Israelites to return to their homeland after generations of exile in Babylon. During

Jesus' time, the hope for a savior who would liberate God's people from the Romans had grown to a fever pitch, so charismatic leaders and teachers wore the title as hopes were pinned on them.

All of this seems strange to us, for we modern Christians save these interchangeable terms for Jesus alone. It might help to think of the original meaning of *christos* as one who is marked. Jesus was marked by God before time began. In the fullness of time, at a time marked by God, Jesus came to earth. His arrival was foretold to Mary, and to Joseph, who made a space for him in their lives, and he appeared on a specific day, a day we have by custom marked on our calendars as December 25. He began his ministry and was quickly marked by authorities as a troublemaker. He was marked for death, a death that would save our lives.

As we consider the Greek letter chi, we can appreciate its shape as an X, the typical symbol across cultures used to mark a spot. We can think about how Jesus was marked to be our savior before time began, and we can consider that Jesus is more than just an idea or even a historical figure, but one who stepped out of eternity into a specific time and place on earth to meet us. In nailing down a place and time, God set a date with us.

"But what about you?" he asked. "Who do you say that I am?" Peter answered, "You are the Messiah." – Mark 8:29

Add a Prayer Practice Draw a small x on your hand. As you go through the day, pay attention to it. Think about the fact that God made a decision to create you and said, "On this day, this child shall be born." Regardless of the circumstances of your birth, you were planned and designed by God.

Let the x remind you that someone (or several someones) looked at you and decided, "That one needs to know about Jesus." They took the time to tell you the story and show you the path. There are those who have chosen to love you.

Jesus promised to be with his followers always. He's not an abstract idea, but a real person who knows you and loves you. You are not alone. Let this mark remind you that you, too, are marked as a follower, named "Christian" after him, a name that carries great weight and responsibility.

How is it with Your Soul?

Psi looks like a trident, and in its early version, the "handle" was not present, so the letter looked like a chicken foot.

Psi makes the "ps" sound. It's not a familiar sound to us, but when we learn that the prefix psi means "false," we can hear it in words like "pseudonym" (false name) and "pseudopod" (an appendage that looks like a foot, but isn't).

Psi begins the word *phuxe*, which means "soul," "life," or "identity." The letter psi has become a symbol for the practice of psychology. We can imagine a psychiatrist wielding the pitchfork psi to poke out our inner thoughts.

We can also imagine the Holy Spirit using the same tool to reveal what's true and what's false. Read the gospels and the ways Jesus challenged the hypocrisy of those who would follow him, and you might wonder how the pitchfork became associated with Satan instead of Jesus. We may be able to mask our true selves from others and hide the truth from the world, but God is not fooled.

Make a Connection   We are often tricked into chasing after false things and losing our souls. Jesus tells a parable of a merchant who discovers a pearl in a shop and sells all he has to buy it. Others might not see the value of the pearl, but he does, and it does not matter to him if he looks foolish giving up everything for it. This is like the Kingdom of God.

Jesus said that whoever wants to save his life will lose it, but whoever loses his life for Jesus' sake will save it. This seems like a paradox, but it helps to know that in the original text, we don't find the usual Greek word for life, *zoe*, we instead find the word *phuxe*, which means not only "life," but also "soul," and "identity." In other words, whoever wants to cling to his self-created identity will lose it, but whoever lets go of his identity for Jesus' sake will find his true self. In Christ and in his gospel, we find our true selves and are able to let go of the false identities we use as defense mechanisms. It takes soul-searching to realize we are even doing this, for most of us have been wearing these masks for a long, long time, so long, in fact, that we've forgotten they are not us.

Those of us who know Christ want to surround ourselves with people who will ask us not just, "How are you?" but, "How is it with your soul?" Early Methodism grew and became strong though small group meetings, during which the faithful asked each other that question. Some people still observe this practice. The original phrase among the Methodists in the 18th century was, "How does your soul prosper?" This question allowed the groups to probe deeply and hold each other accountable on the path of ongoing spiritual growth. In a sense, it allowed them to poke each other with a spiritual pitchfork and sift out the truth.

For whoever wants to save their life will lose it, but whoever loses their life for me and for the gospel will save it. –Matthew 16:25

Add a Prayer Practice No one wants to be poked with a fork, but there was a reason Jesus asked probing questions so often. If it seems threatening, consider what you're protecting.

The spiritually strong will often point to "poking moments" as turning points in their lives. So ask yourself, "How is it with my soul?" Are you in danger of losing your soul, or trading it for something that will ultimately prove to be of little value? How are you spending your time and money? Pitchfork-shaped psi is not a familiar letter to us. Don't be afraid to get to know it.

God is Here

Omega

o as in hold

Egyptian Hebrew Greek Roman

The last letter of the Greek alphabet, omega, is one of the two letters that evolved into our letter "O." Omega literally means "large O," for mega means "large," and the other O letter, omicron, literally means "small O," for micro means "small." Omega makes a long o sound like you're saying "oh," and it begins the word *ode*, which means "here." It also begins the word *ora*, which means "hour," often used in the Bible to signify a specific time. Omega can remind us of God's presence with us here in this very hour.

Omega is open on the bottom, which can remind us that our story with God is open-ended and still being written. Omega also stands firm, declaring a boundary. With God we live in a space that is both full of possibility for the future, but held firm within his boundaries for creation.

Make a Connection Omega stands at the end of the Greek alphabet, providing a hard stop. It's little feet plant into the ground and hold fast. We can imagine God standing firm at the edge of all things, hemming us in, keeping us safe. We cannot get past, we cannot reach a place that is beyond God's ability to love and forgive us. Even when we reach the end of our lives, God is there to receive us and hold us for eternity.

Jesus gives the Great Commission to the disciples, a command for them to continue his work and make disciples. Before he leaves them, he promises that he will be with them always. In the end, God makes his home with mortals. While we may imagine ourselves ascending to heaven on angel's wings, the final scene in Scripture has God coming to us, keeping the promise.

Life doesn't always make sense to us. When God says no and tells us to stop, we often push back, believing our way is the only way and that our will is what should be done. Like Adam and Eve, we eat the forbidden fruit (Genesis 3). Like Sarai who did not trust that God would give her a child as promised, we take matters into our own hands (Genesis 16). Like Job, we resist humility and demand to know why we suffer. The Lord's answer to Job is powerful:

> Where were you when I laid the foundation of the earth? Tell me, if you have understanding. Who determined its measurements? Surely you know! Or who stretched the line upon it? On what were its bases sunk, or who laid its cornerstone when the morning stars sang together and all the heavenly beings shouted for joy? Or who shut in the sea with its doors when it burst out from the womb? – when I made the clouds its garment, and thick darkness its swaddling band, and prescribed bounds for it, and set bars and doors, and said, 'Thus far you shall come, and no farther, and here your proud waves be stopped'? - Job 38:4-11

I am with you always, even to the end of the age.

-Matthew 28:20

Try a Prayer Practice Picture God as the letter omega, a big, bold presence standing his ground, feet firmly planted. God will not let you be moved out of your safe holding place, no matter how much you feel forces pushing and pulling at you. When you feel like your faith is weak and your trust is failing, hear your Creator's strong voice saying to the forces working against you, "This far you shall come, and no farther!" Trust the power that formed the earth. You don't have to fix everything or understand it all right now. Let that be OK. Settle in, safe and secure.

What Space are You In?

> O LORD, you have searched me and known me.
> You know when I sit down and when I rise up;
> you discern my thoughts from far away. You
> search out my path and my lying down and are
> acquainted with all my ways. Even before a
> word is on my tongue, O LORD, you know it
> completely. You hem me in, behind and before,
> and lay your hand upon me. - Psalm 139:1-5

Alpha and omega stand as bookends, each holding things in place with their feet firmly planted. We may feel anxious or unsettled in our lives, but thinking about alpha and omega at either end of the Greek alphabet can remind us of the words of Psalm 139, God hems us in behind and before. We are held.

The more we trust that God is in control, the more we can accept the things that are and be at peace. When situations call for us to stand and push back against injustice, we can have confidence that we are braced. From this position of strength, we can lean into the unknown and into God's unfolding story. What feels unfinished and uncertain is really the perfect place where God has placed us, teaching us, growing us, molding us into the people we were created to be.

Flip back and look at the letters again. Which resonates most with you now? Listen to the Holy Spirit calling to you from the printed words and images, giving you strength. Remember what you know of holiness, home, and heaven. Remember what you know about yourself and your potential. Remember to look deeper and look beyond. Remember that the Holy One is with you.

When Jesus breathed his last breath on the cross, he said, "It is finished." And so we know it is. We know that God has secured the victory over sin and death. When worries and fears bubble up, remind yourself that you exist in a holding place, waiting for God to redeem all things and for the Holy City, the New Jerusalem, to come down from heaven, and for God to make a home among us. The time will come, and no matter where you are, the Kingdom of God is near.

Peace be with you.